STACEY ABRAMS

Voting
Visionary

ANDREA J. LONEY

INTERIOR ILLUSTRATIONS BY
SHELLENE RODNEY

HARPER
An Imprint of HarperCollinsPublishers

www.harpercollinschildrens.com

Library of Congress Control Number: 2021946934

ISBN 978-0-06-314106-3 (pbk) — ISBN 978-0-06-314107-0

Illustrations by Shellene Rodney

Typography by Torborg Davern

22 23 24 25 26   PC/LSCC   10 9 8 7 6 5 4 3 2 1

❖

First Edition

For Grandma Inez and Gran Gran Nannie B—
two beloved daughters of the South who taught us
the power of family, faith, and service.

Contents

STACEY ABRAMS

YOUTH SPEAKER

C-SPAN

LIVE

We the People

The door swung open with a whoosh. Giddy with excitement, ten-year-old Stacey Abrams followed her parents and her big sister into the school building. She made sure to keep her younger sisters and brothers close behind her.

As the Abrams family passed the offices, lockers, and classrooms, Stacey could not stop smiling. She'd waited the whole school day for this moment.

Finally, they reached the gymnasium. The room was all set up, but not for the cheers and roars of a basketball game, the toots and squeaks of a band concert, or the polite applause of a school assembly.

This time, there was the gentle *swish, swish, swish* of curtains opening and closing on the many rows of voting booths filling the gym.

It was Election Day, 1984, in Gulfport, Mississippi.

For the grown-ups, of course. Stacey and the other kids were all too young to vote.

Stacey watched as her parents signed the big book at the front table and received their ballots. All around that gymnasium, folks made their selections and cast their votes for political leaders. Stacey liked how the whole community came together to choose the right people to serve their town, their state, and even the whole country. She knew that her community needed the help.

The people of her Black working-class neighborhood worked very hard, but many of them still struggled to get by. Even though her parents both had college degrees, her mother was an underpaid librarian and her father worked at a shipyard.

From an early age, Stacey saw how unfair the world could be. She wanted to help her community. But would her community ever choose her? Would a whole gymnasium of people ever vote for Stacey Abrams? The thought thrilled her, but it also frightened her.

Back at home, the Abrams family watched the election coverage. The political candidates wore tailored suits and gave big, inspiring speeches to hundreds—even thousands—of people.

Quiet, shy Stacey could not even imagine herself speaking to all those strangers at once. She didn't like being in the spotlight. And those expensive clothes? Her family could never afford that.

But most of all, as she watched the images of politicians flickering on the screen, Stacey noticed that none of them looked anything like her. Most of them were men. Almost all of them were white.

On Election Day 1984, Stacey Abrams was just a young Black girl living in small-town Mississippi with big dreams and a tiny voice.

How could she ever inspire anyone to vote?

CHAPTER 1

Voting Booth Battles, Part 1

Voting was a big deal to Stacey's family. Her parents didn't just wait for the presidential race every four years. They also voted for their governors, mayors, judges, and other local officials. If there was an election, the Abrams family showed up to be counted.

It was important to Carolyn and Robert Abrams that their children saw every aspect of the voting process. Stacey's family could not participate in local elections until the late 1960s. Stacey and her siblings were the first generation of Southern

Black people all born with the right to just walk into a school gym, cast a vote, and walk back out unharmed.

But why?

In 1865, immediately after the end of the Civil War, the United States entered a brief era called Reconstruction. It was supposed to unite the country. The federal government passed laws to protect formerly enslaved Black people and even sent troops to enforce those laws. Black men gained the right to vote, run for public office, own property, and more. They set up communities with flourishing businesses. Some two thousand African Americans held office as elected officials, including sixteen members of the US Congress.

However, many white Southerners despised these changes. After a controversial presidential election in 1876, some Southern lawmakers met with the new president's representatives to strike a deal. In the Compromise of 1877, Southern states agreed to accept the election results, if the federal government agreed to stop protecting Black people in their states. This was the  end of Reconstruction and the beginning of the Jim Crow era.

In the 1870s in Mississippi, where Stacey Abrams's ancestors lived, the Jim Crow era led to new local laws created to erase the legal, economic, and social gains that Black people had made during Reconstruction. If folks in their neighborhoods even talked about voting, they could be attacked by police dogs, arrested, or killed by angry white mobs. Without Black voters' input, politicians continued to pass laws that kept the Black people of the South poor and oppressed for nearly a hundred years.

Both of Stacey Abrams's parents protested and marched for their rights in the 1960s. As a young teen, Robert Abrams was thrown in jail for trying to register Black voters. It took the combined effort, hard work, and sacrifice of many people, including civil rights leaders like future congressman John Lewis, Dr. Martin Luther King, and even President Lyndon Johnson to convince the white people of the United States that Black citizens deserved the right to vote.

The Voting Rights Act of 1965 meant that the states could not stop Black voters with literacy tests, poll taxes, the threat of arrest, or any other forms of voter suppression. But even after that law passed, not everyone trusted those newfound rights.

Who Had the Right to Vote?

When the Constitution was written in 1776, only certain people could vote. Today, most citizens of the United States over the age of eighteen can vote, no matter their gender, race, ethnicity, creed, religion, income level, disability, or primary language. So who could vote and when?

1776: Generally, the only people allowed to vote are white men age twenty-one and over who own property. Some states have religious requirements.

1848: After the Mexican-American War, Mexicans living in new US territories are technically allowed to vote, but most states won't let them.

1856: White males at least twenty-one years old can vote. Restrictions on owning property or practicing a certain religion are eliminated.

1870: After the Civil War, the Fifteenth Amendment grants men of all races the right to vote. Some states create new rules to keep Black, Asian, and other minority men from voting.

1920: With the Nineteenth Amendment, white women are guaranteed the right to vote, but many Black, Native American, Asian, and Hispanic women are still denied that right.

1924: The Snyder Act grants Native Americans the right to vote, but many states refuse to enact it.

1943: Chinese Americans are guaranteed the right to vote after the Chinese Exclusion Act is repealed.

1965: After the civil rights movement, the Voting Rights Act outlaws voter suppression of Black people and other minorities.

1970: After the Vietnam War protests, the Twenty-Sixth Amendment lowers the voting age from twenty-one to eighteen.

1975: The Voting Rights Act is changed so non-English-speaking citizens can also vote.

1982: The Voting Rights Act is changed to accommodate disabled people and voters who cannot read.

2006: Congress renews the Voting Rights Act for twenty-five more years.

2013: The Supreme Court guts the Voting Rights Act by allowing states with a history of discrimination against minorities to create new voting rules with no interference from the federal government. Some Southern states imme-diately set up new laws to restrict mostly minority voters.

Stacey's grandmother once told her about the very first time she voted, a couple of years after the Voting Rights Act was passed in 1965. Her family waited downstairs as she dressed for the big occasion. But when her husband called for her to join them, Stacey's grandmother couldn't leave the bedroom. She was terrified.

No one in her family had been allowed to vote in almost a century. What if angry men showed up at the polls with dogs, guns, and violence? And on top of her fear, Stacey's grandmother felt ashamed that so many people—including her own son—had fought for the right to vote, yet she was still too afraid to leave the house.

Even though Stacey's grandmother was scared to vote that day, she did it anyway. She got herself downstairs and went to the polls with her family. No one attacked them. And she never missed a chance to vote after that.

CHAPTER 2

Education, Faith, and Family

Stacey's parents grew up in the small, poor, segregated town of Hattiesburg, Mississippi, and became high school sweethearts. Carolyn, the oldest of seven kids, was the first person in her family to graduate from high school. She was also the class valedictorian. Robert was the first man in his family to graduate from college. It wasn't easy for him—he had an undiagnosed learning disorder, and his teachers did not expect him to go far in life.

Hattiesburg

The couple moved to Wisconsin so Carolyn could get her library sciences degree. In 1970, they welcomed their first daughter, Andrea. Stacey arrived on December 9, 1973. The next year, their daughter Leslie was born.

When they returned to their home state, the Abramses knew that choosing the right neighborhood could change their family's future. In Gulfport, Mississippi, they found the least expensive part of town that still had a great school district. It meant that they needed to rent a house in the poorest part of that district. But it also meant that their children could have better opportunities.

After that the rest of their children followed quickly: their sons, Richard and Walter, and finally their youngest daughter, Jeanine. With six kids, the Abramses had a big brood, but not a big bank account. Luckily, they also had a big plan for their family's future. It was three simple steps—their Trinity of Success.

Stacey's parents gave their children three rules:

1. Go to school
2. Go to church
3. Take care of each other

Go to School

Stacey's mother described their family as "genteel poor." For her, it meant that while they didn't have much money, she still wanted them to be well-rounded. The family watched educational and cultural programs on PBS. If Stacey had questions, her mother directed her to find the answers in the dictionary. And all three older sisters joined the Girl Scouts.

While the kids in her neighborhood were Black, Stacey's schoolmates were mostly white. But Stacey studied hard and did well. She also attended special classes for gifted students in a different school on the richer side of town.

From an early age, Stacey saw how families with

more money could get access to better opportunities. Meanwhile, the poor students—who were just as smart or even smarter—often got scraps and leftovers. It didn't seem fair to her.

Go to Church

Church was a huge part of the Abramses' family life. Sitting in the pews, the family listened to sermons about African Americans leaning on their faith to deal with poverty, injustice, and the endless cruelty of slavery and Jim Crow laws. Faith was not just about going to services for them. For the Abramses, their faith was all about being *of service* to others.

On Saturdays, the family volunteered at soup kitchens, homeless shelters, and other places where

people had been forgotten by society. The Abramses did not have much money, but they shared what they had with people who needed it—one sandwich, one reading lesson, and one act of kindness at a time.

Take Care of Each Other

While their parents went to work, the Abrams kids were responsible for each other. Stacey's older sister, Andrea, took care of baby Jeanine. Her younger sister Leslie watched over their youngest brother, Walter. And Stacey looked after their brother Richard. Every morning, the older siblings made sure that the younger siblings were dressed, fed, and ready for school.

The Trinity of Success worked well for the Abrams family. Stacey excelled in school. And she did so well in the Scouts, she was selected to attend a national Girl Scout conference in Scottsdale, Arizona. The Abrams family was thrilled. However, some people in her troop were outraged. They did not think that a Black girl like Stacey should represent the state of Mississippi at the conference.

Even though Stacey's parents couldn't travel with her, she was ready for her opportunity to shine. But when she got to the airport, there was a problem. Somebody had changed her plane ticket. Someone did not want her going to that conference.

Too bad—Stacey wasn't going to let them stop her. Even though she was just a kid, she got it sorted out and took her very first plane ride across the country. She may have been quiet and shy, but she had something to say. And she had a right to be there.

Jim Crow Era Voter Suppression Techniques

- **poll taxes**—a voting fee that could equal a day's or even a week's wages

- **literacy tests**—first used to keep Irish-Catholic immigrants from voting, these laws required people to read and interpret complicated legal passages in order to vote. Some even included unanswerable questions like "How many bubbles are there in a bar of soap?"

- **grandfather laws**—laws that let poor or uneducated white people skip the tests and taxes if their father or grandfather had been allowed to vote

- **vagrancy laws**—laws that made it illegal for Black people to be outside without a purpose (like going to work) approved by the authorities

- **intimidation**—threatening violence, harm, or death to Black people who tried to vote. Sometimes white townspeople would even murder African American voters as a warning to the rest of the Black people in the area.

CHAPTER 3

The Power of the Pen

Stacey loved books. She could lose herself for hours in a good adventure or spy novel. She also had a way with words, writing essays, poetry, and songs. At age fourteen, she poured her feelings into her very first novel, titled *My Diary of Angst*.

Stacey's writing skills didn't go unnoticed. In middle school, she won a big citywide essay contest. The prize was a ribbon and fifty dollars. Excited to receive her prize, Stacey went to pick up her award. But the

white woman in charge of the contest didn't believe that Stacey wrote the essay. As everyone in the school lobby watched, the woman refused to give Stacey her prize.

But Stacey hadn't done anything wrong. She'd earned that prize. The woman demanded that Stacey show her photo identification. But she was only an eighth grader—how would she have a driver's license? The woman treated Stacey as if she had no right to expect something that was already hers. And secretly, Stacey worried that she might be right.

It wasn't the first time that a grown-up didn't believe in her skills, her intelligence, or her right to be there. In fact, it happened a lot. And it hurt. It also made her feel nervous to take big risks.

But things changed after Stacey turned fifteen. Her parents decided to study divinity and become United Methodist ministers. The family moved to Atlanta, Georgia. Stacey enrolled in a performing arts school. She wrote poetry for the school literary magazine and joined the theater program. As a junior, Stacey did so well on her college prep tests, she got into the world-famous Telluride summer program on the campus of Cornell University in New York. Which was great . . .

. . . until she got there.

Stacey knew that she was a good student and a good writer. But the kids at Telluride had done things she'd never even dreamed of. One was already a published poet. Some had traveled all over the world. Some spoke different languages like French and Farsi. They discussed books she'd never even heard of. When Stacey finally tried to talk about her favorite television shows, the other kids just stared at her.

Stacey could not compete with these kids.

When she called home in tears, her father told her she had to get used to not being the smartest person in the room. So Stacey made the best of the situation. She listened carefully to the other students. She watched how they carried themselves. She learned from them. And when she returned to Georgia, she also carried herself with confidence and poise. The Telluride experience began as a disaster for Stacey, but in the end, it gave her the opportunity to grow in new and exciting ways.

Soon after Telluride, Stacey volunteered for a local political candidate. While typing one of his speeches, she fixed some of his wording. When the politician saw her work, he hired her to write more speeches, and Stacey Abrams became a political speechwriter at the age of seventeen.

Stacey graduated as the valedictorian

of her class. At the end of the school year, the high school valedictorians were invited to a party at the Georgia governor's mansion. Stacey and her parents took the bus there, ready to celebrate with the rest of the families. But before they could enter, a security guard stopped them. He refused to believe that Stacey belonged in that event with those high-achieving students and their families. By then, the bus was already long gone. On a day that should have been a joyful achievement for Stacey, racism ruined the party again.

By that point, Stacey was ready to leave the South. She'd applied to a few colleges up north—Sarah Lawrence and Vassar in New York, and Swarthmore in Pennsylvania, But her mother had other plans for her: Spelman College.

What Are Historically Black Colleges and Universities (HBCUs)?

After the Civil War ended in 1865, several historically Black colleges and universities were founded. These schools provided Black men and women with the education they needed to help their communities by becoming doctors, lawyers, politicians, educators, ministers, scientists, businesspeople, and more.

By 1930, there were 121 HBCUs. The Civil Rights Act of 1964 opened higher education to students of all races, and Black students could finally attend many colleges that were previously closed to them. Today, 101 HBCUs remain, including these famous schools with their notable alumni:

Fisk University (Nashville, TN): author W. E. B. Du Bois, journalist Ida B. Wells, poet Nikki Giovanni

Howard University (Washington, DC): Vice President Kamala Harris, Supreme Court Justice Thurgood Marshall

Morehouse College (Atlanta, GA): Rev. Dr. Martin Luther King Jr., filmmaker Spike Lee, and more Rhodes Scholars than any HBCU

North Carolina A&T State University (Greensboro, NC): astronaut Dr. Ronald McNair, and more African American engineers than any other HBCU

Spelman College (Atlanta, GA): politician Stacey Abrams, author Alice Walker

Tennessee State University (Nashville, TN): billionaire talk show host Oprah Winfrey

Texas Southern University (Houston, TX): TV host and athlete Michael Strahan

Tuskegee University (Tuskegee, AL): Founded by educator Booker T. Washington, it was the workplace of inventor George Washington Carver. Famous alumni—the Tuskegee

Airmen, and NASA engineer and inventor of the Super Soaker Lonnie Johnson.

West Virginia State University (Institute, WV): NASA mathematician Katherine Johnson

Xavier University of Louisiana (New Orleans, LA): graduates more Black medical school candidates than any other university in the United States

It was the last school Stacey wanted to attend for her big college experience. It was an all-Black and all-female school, and worst of all, it was right in her hometown of Atlanta. Stacey wanted to explore more of the world. What if she met a cute boy? Stacey had only been allowed to date for less than a year, but she wanted to keep her options open.

Still, Stacey put the names of the four colleges into a cup and pulled them out. Spelman came out three times.

When Stacey finally visited the Spelman College campus, she was astounded. Accomplished, sophisticated, highly educated, and even wealthy young Black women were everywhere. They were preparing to become powerful forces in the world. Stacey couldn't wait to join them.

Stacey Abrams was ready to launch her college career at Spelman College.

But she was not ready for her first semester at Spelman to launch her career in politics.

CHAPTER 4

From Personal to Political

Even though Spelman was only twenty minutes away from her high school, starting college felt like running away to a whole new world. Stacey had never been around so many well-to-do Black people before. Their lives were so different from hers. She didn't always understand the slang, music, and dances that her classmates enjoyed. Stacey had hoped that going to a school full of smart Black girls would make her feel more at home, but she was feeling like an outsider yet again.

Even more troublesome for Stacey were the costs involved with going to college. In high school, she slept and ate at home. The school provided students with free books and classes. But in college, she struggled to find ways to pay for everything— tuition, housing, food, transportation, and more. Coming from a well-educated family without much money, Stacey knew far more about academics than finances. And she wasn't the only student with that problem. When she heard that the school was considering raising tuition and fees, she decided she had to speak up for the students who were struggling.

She found out where the school's board of trustees would be meeting, and then Stacey asked the president of the college to let her sit in the session. Once she got inside, she realized three very important things:

1. she'd never been in a board meeting before,
2. she was wearing jeans and a T-shirt while everyone else was dressed in expensive suits; and
3. she had no idea what to do next.

Thankfully, some kind board members sat her down and showed her their notebooks. They told her about the decisions they were making about the school's finances. For the first time, Stacey learned about the inner workings of the *business* of education—how much it costs to run a school and how that affects the price of tuition.

The reports and spreadsheets unveiling Spelman's cash flow secrets fascinated Stacey. She attended more meetings and even earned her own meeting notebook.

Stacey also spent time with Dr. Johnnetta Cole, the president of Spelman College.

She attended fancy gala events, listened in on fundraising calls, and learned more about school politics. The more Stacey learned about how money worked, the more she wanted to help her fellow students too.

This inspired Stacey Abrams to run for her first political position—vice president of the student body at Spelman. Unlike the students who hung out with lots of friends in sororities and other groups on campus, Stacey only had a few close confidants. She didn't have many connections. But Stacey had plans. She'd made banners, posters, and everything. She had it all worked out.

And then, the night before she was supposed to

set up for the election, Stacey found out that her roommate had taken her campaign materials and showed them to her competitor. Stacey was crushed but not defeated. Now she was forced to reach out to other people for help. She came up with all new campaign slogans and gear. It wasn't easy! She lost some friends, but she won that first election. And she learned how to lean on other people, even when she wanted to do everything all by herself.

Still, Stacey was happiest spending time on her studies and student government. But then her boyfriend, who was only the second boy she'd ever dated, broke up with her. He complained that she was too focused on her work. Stacey was devastated. Dating was still new to her, and romance was confusing.

That painful experience inspired Stacey. She spent that Friday night in the computer lab of her school, creating a big spreadsheet of all the things she wanted to accomplish in her life. It had four columns listing the year, her age, the job, and what she would do in that job. As other students partied, Stacey planned her future.

Your Spreadsheet

Have you thought what you might want to be
doing when you are eighteen, twenty-eight,
and thirty-eight?

How about when you are fifty-eight?

Or even eighty-eight?

She decided that by age twenty-four, she would write an exciting, best-selling spy novel. She'd already read books by Black suspense writers, so this seemed reasonable. Then, by age  thirty, she would be the millionaire head of a corporation, maybe like Oprah. Lastly, by age thirty-five,

she would be elected the mayor of Atlanta, Georgia. At the time, this item seemed the least likely to happen. In 1992, no Black woman had ever led a big city in the US. But Stacey figured that if she started working on this dream at age twenty, she'd be ready to make it happen in fifteen years.

Setting up this spreadsheet made Stacey feel like she had a clearer view of her future. It gave her a vision of how amazing her life could be, even if she didn't reach all those goals in the exact way she'd imagined them. She felt that if she just stayed on her path, everything would be okay.

But then an event almost three thousand miles away changed the course of her life and her legacy.

CHAPTER 5

Activism and Access

In April 1992, after a highly publicized trial, a jury in Los Angeles acquitted four police officers accused of brutally beating a Black man named Rodney King. Even with video evidence, the officers were found not guilty on all charges. This verdict sparked the Los Angeles Uprising, also known as the Los Angeles Riots.

From the palm tree–studded streets of LA to the skyscraper-laden island of Manhattan, African

Americans and their allies were outraged to see yet another Black man denied justice in the face of police brutality. Protests began in many major cities, and Atlanta was no exception. As a student at a historically Black college, Stacey noticed three major reactions from those around her:

1. Silent marches

Following in the peaceful footsteps of Dr. Martin Luther King Jr., Stacey and some other students from local HBCUs quickly organized and led a silent and peaceful march to city hall.

2. Violent protests

Nearby, in the poor housing projects, some young people reacted with anger and violence. Stacey understood their rage at waiting for decades to see real change in the treatment of African Americans.

3. Studying even harder

On campus, some students simply focused on their final exams. Stacey understood that many

HBCU students chose to fight injustice by succeeding in school and then becoming lawyers, doctors, judges, businesspeople, and other professionals who might have the power to influence the system.

However, the Atlanta police saw no difference between the protesters outside the colleges destroying property and the students inside the colleges cramming for exams. The police poured into both the housing projects and the school campuses, lobbing tear gas canisters and terrifying local residents and students alike.

Television news reports also described young Black people as being violent and dangerous. The reporters didn't

address the reason behind the anger. They didn't discuss concerns that the "not guilty" verdict would trigger even more violence against Black people.

Stacey could not stand by and watch her classmates, her neighborhood, and herself be misrepresented that way. She called the television stations to protest. She got the students in her college dorm to call as well.

Soon, a TV producer invited Stacey to a community town hall meeting. Stacey was in awe of the legendary Mayor Maynard Jackson, the first African American mayor of Atlanta, as he shared how unhappy he was with the Rodney King verdict. But when the mayor justified sending the police after all the young people in both the housing projects and the school campuses, Stacey became furious. She asked him what he'd actually done to help the

youth of Atlanta, many of whom were feeling hopeless, impoverished, and forgotten.

Mayor Jackson promised to think about what she'd said. Soon, Stacey joined the mayor's Office of Youth Services. With access to the inner workings of local government, Stacey hoped to give a voice to those who had none.

Meanwhile, Stacey continued to fight injustice. She and other Spelman students protested the Georgia State flag, which since the 1950s, had featured an image of the Confederate flag.

What Was the Confederacy?

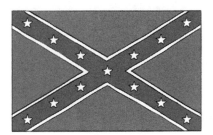

The Confederate States of America was a treasonous breakaway government of eleven Southern states. It lasted from 1861 to 1865.

When Abraham Lincoln campaigned for the presidency in 1860, he vowed to end the horror of slavery. However, Southern states were dependent on free labor to fund their way of life and to promote their devotion to white supremacy—their belief that white people should rule over others. While Black people were enslaved mostly by wealthy plantation owners, both rich and poor whites in the South benefited from the institution.

After President Lincoln was elected in 1861, eleven states seceded from—or left—the United States: South Carolina, Mississippi, Florida, Alabama, Georgia, Louisiana, Texas, Virginia, Arkansas, North Carolina, and Tennessee.

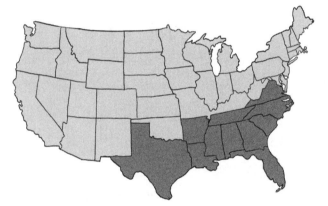

The Confederacy struggled to fight the larger, better equipped, and more organized Union armies from the North. They struggled to sell plantation crops overseas as the Union army blocked their seaports. They even struggled within their own organization, because the individual states did not want to work together. After hundreds of thousands of Southerners died fighting for the Confederacy, it came to an end in 1865.

Around the 1920s, the last Civil War veterans began to pass away. Fans and descendants of Confederate veterans

honored them by building monuments. They also did this to reaffirm their devotion to white supremacy. This movement led to the resurgence of the Ku Klux Klan, or KKK, a domestic terrorist group founded in 1866 that targets African Americans and other minorities. Even more Confederate monuments were built as a response to the civil rights movement—almost a hundred years after the Confederacy ended. Some were even built in states that had never fought in the Civil War!

Two months after the 2020 election, hundreds of violent supporters of President Donald Trump led a deadly attack on Congress, which was completing the steps for newly elected President Joseph Biden to take office. Television stations, websites, and newspapers all over the world showed a white supremacist waving the Confederate flag right in the Capitol building.

Unfortunately, over 150 years after the end of the Confederacy, some people in the United States are still devoted to a doomed movement that ripped the nation in two.

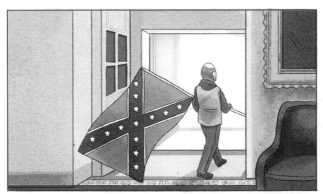

Many people believed that symbols of a traitor-
ous movement against the United States had no
place on a state flag. It was especially insulting to
the Black Georgians. The governor wouldn't discuss
the issue with Stacey and her classmates, so the students took action. After Stacey filed for the proper
permit, they burned the Georgia state flag and its
Confederate symbolism, right on the steps of the
Georgia capitol building.

Suddenly, shy Stacey Abrams found herself in
the spotlight. She was asked to speak at the thirti-
eth anniversary of Martin Luther King's March on

Washington for Jobs and Freedom in DC. Thousands of marchers stretched from the stage to the reflecting pool of the National Mall. Her heart racing, she gave a stirring speech on jobs, peace, and justice. She asked the crowd to see the young people of America as a solution to the country's problems. She said that the youth of America were ready to make the US a better place for everyone.

Her speech was brief, passionate, and followed by thunderous applause.

CHAPTER 6

Stacey in the House

With newfound confidence, Stacey decided to dream big. After graduating from Spelman, she finally left her hometown to earn a master's degree at the University of Texas in Austin. Next, she attended Yale Law School in chilly, snowy Connecticut. All throughout her graduate and law school years, Stacey met people from different races, countries, social classes, and political persuasions. She learned from them. They expanded her view of the world.

In her third year of law school, Stacey decided to pursue a dream from her big spreadsheet. She wrote a spy thriller novel that combined her passion for exciting James Bond movies with her love of dreamy soap operas like *General Hospital*. But the publishers she contacted doubted there was a market for books about Black spies written by a Black woman.

So in her next draft, Stacey made the two spies fall in love. The publishers loved it and the book sold! Under the pen name of Selena Montgomery, Stacey Abrams went on to publish several popular romance  novels about African American professionals.

After law school, Stacey landed a dream job as a tax attorney in an Atlanta law firm. Stacey loved tax law—tracking the different streams of money that drove the federal, state, and local governments fascinated her. But it wasn't just her fancy office or her hefty paycheck that made this job great. In addition

to the regular work for her law firm, Stacey served nonprofit organizations that helped the people and causes she believed in. This job fit perfectly into the Abrams family Trinity of Success: Stacey was able to use her education to be of service to others and to help her family financially as well.

After working with Shirley Franklin, the first African American female mayor of Atlanta, Stacey Abrams became a city attorney. But even though Stacey loved the job and learned so much from Mayor Franklin, there were still many injustices that Stacey wanted to address. She needed to find a bigger position in government.

What Are Taxes?

Taxes are the money the government takes from companies and people to pay for big projects. Taxes pay for little things, like trash cans on street corners, and big things like public schools, roads and bridges, and even sending scientific missions to space. Income taxes come from the wages that someone earns at work. Sales tax takes a percentage of a purchase bought at a store. Other taxes may come as fees added to 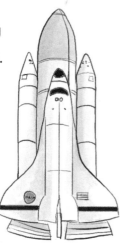 the price of a service, like a cell phone bill, or based on where you live, like property taxes.

How can taxes help or hurt communities?

Taxes can be used to help people by funding ways to make their community a better, cleaner, and safer place to live. Politicians look at the amount of taxes that comes in and make a budget to decide what should be done with the money. One reason that voting is so important is that voting chooses the people who decide where the tax dollars go. When people can't vote, they don't get a say in electing people who will consider their needs.

So Stacey decided to run for public office. She wasn't as connected as some of the other candidates and couldn't rely on recommendations or endorsements from well-known politicians.

But Stacey knew a great deal about fundraising and organizing. She also reached out to everyone who might be able to help her cause, even people who most candidates would forget about or ignore. Ultimately, Stacey Abrams beat two experienced politicians to serve in the Georgia House of Representatives.

STACEY ABRAMS
D-89

Why State and Local Elections Affect Most People More than National Elections

Many people think of elections as the big nationwide presidential races that happen every four years. But elections for the Senate and the House of Representatives happen every two years. State and local elections can happen every year, and they may have the most impact on people's lives.

Federal laws apply throughout the United States and in every state. These laws affect things like:

- immigration
- civil rights and protection from discrimination
- fighting foreign wars

The US has fifty states as well as commonwealths and territories like Puerto Rico and the District of Columbia (DC). They all have their own individual state laws that may include things like:

- criminal laws
- gun control laws
- public assistance and welfare
- health care
- employment

Within each state, commonwealth, or territory are individual counties, townships, cities, tribal lands, or villages. They have their own laws and rules too, which may include things like:

- how school districts operate
- where businesses, homes, and schools are located
- when the trash is picked up

Most of the laws that impact our day-to-day lives start at the state, county, city, and local levels. This is why it is important to vote in every election.

Stacey leaned on her strengths and did her best to help the people of Georgia. She listened. She learned. She met with her colleagues one-on-one to discuss important issues. In just four years, she became the minority leader in the Georgia State House of Representatives. That meant she was the head of the political party with fewer members who could vote on bills. So Stacey learned how to work with both Democrats and Republicans to get big things done, like protecting the people of Georgia from huge tax hikes and saving an important scholarship program for Georgia college students.

The demographics in Georgia were changing as more people moved to the Peach State from across the country and around the world. Many of the newcomers were under the age of thirty-five, people of color, and unmarried women. Stacey started the New Georgia Project to make sure that all the people who lived in the state had a voice. Her organization

went to churches, colleges, and neighborhoods to educate Georgians on the political process and to register them to vote.

Stacey helped many people across the state with the New Georgia Project. Hundreds of thousands of folks registered to vote through her organization.

However, many injustices still faced the people of Georgia in health care, jobs, and more. Stacey wanted to do more to help, but she needed an even bigger role in government to do it.

So Stacey Abrams decided to run for governor. If she won, she would be the first Black female governor in US history.

But would people vote for Stacey?

CHAPTER 7

Voting Booth Battles, Part 2

From the start of her run for governor of the state of Georgia, Stacey knew she'd face some serious obstacles. Many people said that Georgia was not ready for a female governor *or* a Black governor, but especially not a Black female governor. Even some of Stacey's friends and colleagues doubted that the rest of the state was ready for that kind of change.

Stacey didn't let that stop her, though. She continued to work with different organizations to get out the vote. She didn't invest as much in TV and print advertising campaigns as some of the other candidates. Instead, Stacey and her supporters went out to meet the voters at their homes, schools, churches,

and other community hubs. Many folks said that no politicians had ever reached out to them before. They were not considered "important" voters, so the other candidates had focused elsewhere.

Stacey's campaign fanned out across the state, meeting with different communities, holding town halls, listening to people's needs, and sharing their smiles. And even though she was still a quiet and private person, Stacey's faith and passion for fairness drove her to crisscross the state with her message. Stacey wanted to make sure that the people of her state knew that she heard their problems and she had solutions.

Stacey Abrams shined on the national stage. Everyone was talking about the Georgia governor's race. But not everyone was saying nice things.

Sometimes political candidates try to make each other look bad by exposing their opponent's personal issues. And Stacey had a big one. Stacey's youngest brother, Walter—the sweet, funny sibling who was always the first to call her on her birthday—struggled with bipolar disorder and drug addiction. For years, he'd cycled in and out of prison with these issues. Would people think less of Stacey because of this?

Stacey knew her opponents would mention Walter. But the Abrams family's Trinity of Success included taking care of their siblings. So she handled this situation not by hiding it, but by sharing it. Often.

Stacey told voters what it meant for her to have a loved one with mental health problems. She talked about how drug and legal troubles often followed people with untreated mental illnesses. All around the state and the country, voters heard these stories and felt even more connected to Stacey. Some also had family members with similar difficulties. Some just admired her honesty. Stacey talked about how the system can make it hard for people to recover from these issues. Then she shared her solutions.

Her hard work and honesty paid off. Stacey Abrams won the primary and became the first Black woman in US history to be the party candidate for a governorship.

From there she faced Georgia Secretary of State Brian Kemp, who she'd worked with for years. In the House of Representatives, she'd watched him use his position to kick 1.4 million Georgians off the voting rolls, close polling centers, and use other methods to prevent millions of eligible voters from ever casting a ballot. Kemp was determined to help the Republican party hold on to power in Georgia, no matter how much the demographics of the state had changed.

Modern Methods of Voter Suppression

These days, voters don't worry as much about police attacking them with water cannons, angry dogs, and billy clubs when they go to vote. But modern voters can still be kept from voting by other means:

- **gerrymandering:** redrawing the boundaries around the voting maps to force a specific outcome in the elections

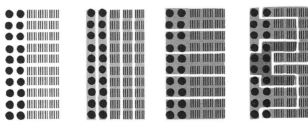

- **poll closures:** closing polling locations so people have to walk or drive farther to vote, or so remaining locations will be crowded

- **voter roll purges:** removing people who are eligible to vote from the list of registered voters.

This can happen when voter rolls are updated to remove people who have moved or died, who are listed more than once, or who are ineligible to vote.

- **unreasonably strict voter ID laws:** requiring ID that some voters have no way to get, like birth certificates from senior citizens who were born at home

- **misinformation campaigns:** using media messages to intentionally give voters the wrong information about an election or candidate so they either miss the election or vote for the wrong candidate

- **underfunding elections:** understaffing and not training poll workers, not fixing broken voting machines or providing proper voting materials

- **combining precincts:** cramming different polling places together, which creates long lines and confusion

- **voter intimidation:** threatening voters with harassment by the police, immigration, or others; also, employers who discourage employees from voting

- **"government errors":** frequent unexplained and sometimes unresolved problems with processing registrations or votes

- **fueling voter apathy:** discouraging people from voting by making the entire process as difficult as possible

Usually midterm races—elections halfway through presidential terms—don't get huge attention. But this election drove people from all over Georgia to get out and vote. Many voted for the very first time. The lines at polling places lasted for hours, especially in majority Black counties. In some cases the waits were due to broken voting machines, or machines with missing power cords. In others, such large crowds had turned out to vote, the polling centers were overwhelmed. Still, many folks stayed in line. They knew they had a right to vote, and they knew that voting gave them a voice.

When the time came for her to cast her own vote, news cameras followed Stacey, her family, and her supporters to the polls. She proudly walked to the table to sign in, just as she'd done in countless elections before. Just as her parents had done when she watched them sign in to vote back when she was a schoolchild.

But there was a hitch.

The woman at the table told Stacey that she couldn't vote because the record said she'd already mailed in her ballot. Stacey knew that she had not. With television cameras beaming their images all over the country, the poll workers became anxious.

After years of battling voter suppression, Stacey had seen this situation before. She calmly told them where to check and how to fix the problem. With everything sorted out, Stacey could finally vote for herself and for others on the ballot.

But if this sort of issue could almost prevent someone like the Democratic candidate for governor from voting in her own election, what was happening to the ordinary people who tried to vote? Would they know how to make sure that their ballot counted? How many other Georgians that day were also told that they could not vote?

CHAPTER 8

Broken Dreams and Broader Horizons

Something was wrong.

As Stacey and her team watched the election returns come in, it was clear that while she'd gotten many votes, she was still trailing Brian Kemp by a small amount. But that was not what she was worried about. The real problem was that her campaign's Voter Protection Hotline was ringing nonstop. Thousands and thousands of calls came in from voters, who, like Stacey herself, had not been able to walk in, cast their ballot, and leave without some sort of trouble.

Four million ballots were cast in that election. Stacey's team collected at least forty thousand stories of voter suppression.

Stacey's team investigated the suppressed votes, but in the end, Brian Kemp had just enough votes to win the election without having to face her again in a tie-breaking runoff election. And since Brian Kemp was both the Republican candidate AND the Secretary of State, it was up to him to make sure he'd run the election fairly.

GEORGIA GOVERNOR

GENERAL ELECTION

R

BRIAN KEMP ✓ 50.2%
1,978,408

D

STACEY ABRAMS 48.8%
1,923,685

So of course, he won.

Still, Stacey did not concede the race. While she acknowledged that Kemp would be the governor of Georgia, she still wanted to fight for the tens of thousands of Georgians whose voices were silenced because their votes were not counted.

After the loss, Stacey went to bed. The next morning, her brother Richard, who'd grown up to be a social worker, brought her breakfast. He took care of her just as she'd looked after him when he was little. Stacey needed time to mourn the end of her campaign. So

she read romance novels, ate ice cream, and watched her favorite television shows for ten days.

And then she got back to work.

For Stacey, the hardest thing about that election loss was the obvious unfairness of it all. Even if she challenged Kemp on every rotten thing he'd done during the race, it still wouldn't solve the biggest problem.

The whole system of voting in Georgia was broken. It was far too easy to deny people's voices. And while the voter suppression in Georgia was directed specifically at Black and brown communities, the broken system was not good for anyone anywhere. Not if they wanted to live in a truly democratic republic.

So Stacey launched two new organizations: Fair Count and Fair Fight.

Fair Count was created to ensure that everyone was included in the upcoming 2020 Census. How can a county know how many voting machines they'll need if they don't know how many people live there? Meanwhile, Fair Fight worked to close the legal loopholes that allowed states like Georgia to prevent over a million people from voting.

What Is the Census and What Does the Census Do?

The census is a simple survey that the United States government uses to count the entire population and to gather basic information about everyone in the country. The US Constitution requires this count to take place once every ten years. Sent directly to homes through mail, online, or in person, it asks how many people are staying in the home, and the gender, age, and race of each person.

The census counts all people, including US citizens, immigrants, elderly people, undocumented people, and children.

What does the government do with the information from the census?

Federal, state, and local governments decide how much money goes to communities based on population totals and other information from the census. With this data, they choose how much to spend on schools, parks, libraries, hospitals, roads, public transportation, public safety, and more.

Businesses use this information to decide where to put their stores, offices, factories, and even new homes. It also helps companies know where to look for new workers.

Also, the federal government uses the census to decide how many seats to give each location in the US House of Representatives, whose members serve as the voices of the residents of each state.

When people do not fill out the census, their communities might not get their fair share of resources. The areas that are undercounted may also get fewer funds than they need for their population.

Who tends to be undercounted on the census? People who move homes frequently, renters, people in single-parent homes, people of color, immigrants, undocumented people, people in rural areas, people with low incomes, houseless people, and small children.

For Stacey, fairness was the only way to move forward. She partnered with organizations all over the country to bring the work of Fair Count and Fair Fight nationwide. Stacey was fighting for the voices of all the voters in the United States of America to be heard.

Stacey Abrams's astounding campaign for governor scared many Republicans, conservatives, and other supporters of President Trump. For decades they had found ways to suppress the votes of people of color, young people, and other liberal or Democratic voters so conservatives could stay in power. Even though Kemp managed to win the governorship, Stacey had led hundreds of thousands of Georgia voters into the light of full citizenship. The chances of these newly empowered voters going back into the shadows for the next election was slim.

Stacey Abrams was ready to make sure that the United States would have freer and fairer elections in 2020. And then, just eight months before one of the most important elections in US history, something suddenly changed every aspect of life for people all over the planet.

It was the novel coronavirus, also known as COVID-19.

In early 2020, this unusual new disease quickly spread across the world, killing people at a terrifying rate. At first, scientists did not understand how it worked or even how people got it. As hundreds of thousands of people got sick and even died from the mysterious virus, everyday life and business slowed to a halt.

Compared to most other countries, the United States had an even bigger problem. President Trump and his supporters did not think the virus was real, or at least believed it wasn't that serious. Scientists

tried to help by sharing new discoveries about the coronavirus as soon as they discovered them. But the president and his supporters shared misinformation, confusion, and lies that only helped to spread the virus to even more people.

Politicians across the country needed to make decisions to protect the public from the deadly disease. Some chose not to. Georgia's governor  Kemp was one of the Republicans who made light of the virus. He even attacked the mayors of the cities that did try to pass laws and rules to keep their people safe, like Atlanta mayor Keisha Lance Bottoms.

How Some State Laws Were Created to Get Around Federal Laws

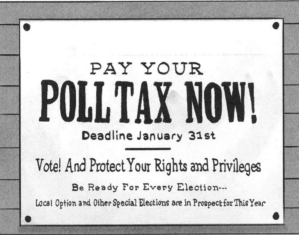

PAY YOUR
POLL TAX NOW!
Deadline January 31st

Vote! And Protect Your Rights and Privileges

Be Ready For Every Election---

Local Option and Other Special Elections are in Prospect for This Year

The Constitution gives citizens the right to vote. But it also gives state and local authorities the power to run those elections. So even though Congress could give a group of people the right to vote, they couldn't do much if the state or town said no. And if people cannot vote, they have no say in which laws get passed.

After the Civil War, when the Thirteenth, Fourteenth, and Fifteenth Amendments granted Black people basic human rights of freedom, citizenship, and the right to vote, Southern states created many new state and local laws, referred to as Jim Crow laws or "black codes" to deny those rights. In fact, the Jim Crow laws made it easier to:

- arrest Black people for minor offenses and give them harsher sentences

- provide Black people with worse treatment in education, housing, medical care, legal matters, banking, and the workplace

REST ROOMS
WHITE   COLORED

- deny African Americans the ability to vote against these Jim Crow laws

Jim Crow laws were never voted for by Congress or ordered by the president, but they have affected the lives and legacies of millions of Americans.

How Some Local Laws Were Created to Get Around State Laws

During the coronavirus pandemic, the federal government refused to take many actions that could have prevented Americans from sickness and death, so it was up to the states to protect their people. Many Republican governors like Georgia governor Brian Kemp wanted to please business owners, conservatives, and President Trump. So he forced some businesses to stay open despite the risks to their employees and customers.

But not all the local leaders of Georgia went along with this plan. Mayors like Keisha Lance

Bottoms, the African American female mayor of Atlanta, worked hard to encourage her residents to stay safe inside, wear masks for safety, and take the pandemic seriously. Governor Kemp and Mayor Bottoms disagreed on the best way to take care of Georgians. He even sued her for requiring the people of Atlanta to wear masks in public.

Across the country, state and local lawmakers debated the best way to handle the pandemic. Since the federal government had failed to take care of its people, it was up to the state government. But if the state government also chose not to take care of its people, sometimes local city, village, and tribal governments did their best to keep people safe.

This is another reason why voting matters at every level—elections allow communities to choose who would care for people and businesses in a crisis.

Many Americans were outraged by this behavior. They did not want to be governed by people who did not look out for their health and well-being. They wanted to replace the president, as well as some congresspeople, governors, mayors, and other politicians. But the only way that they could do that was to vote. And because of the coronavirus, voting in person had become a dangerous activity that could lead to sickness or even death.

But Stacey and her partners had a plan.

CHAPTER 9

Voting Booth Battles, Part 3

The Democratic party pushed to make voting by mail universal. Some states had used mail-in voting or absentee ballots for many years. Military servicemembers, citizens overseas, and even college students have used mail-in voting.

But the Republicans and Trump supporters knew that mail-in voting would be a problem for them. The president even said that if everyone in America was allowed to vote, the Republicans would never win

another election. This was because, instead of promoting ideas that would make people choose to vote for them, the Republicans often decided to make it harder for some voters—especially people of color—to vote them out of office.

The Democrats did what they could to encourage all Americans to vote early by mail. This way there would be less chance of large groups of people being forced to wait in crowded spaces to vote, which could spread more disease. Republicans fought these measures in many ways including legal challenges. A Trump-appointed postmaster general even slowed down the entire US Postal Service by dismantling machines, locking or removing mailboxes, and disrupting mail services across the country.

The census also suffered during this period, as many people were afraid to open their doors to strangers who might come to collect information. The questionnaire was put online so that anyone who had

an internet connection could take it, but some did not have access to a computer or internet services, so they could not be counted. Without an accurate census count, communities across the country could suffer from a lack of important resources.

Partnering with organizations nationwide, Stacey Abrams and her supporters worked around all these obstacles. She leaned on the expertise of many people to help get out the vote and to help people be counted. She also relied on young folks who understood how to use social media and other technology to help Fair Fight and Fair Count to reach people both online and in person.

In the end, the 2020 presidential election saw the largest voter turnout in US history. Former vice president Joe Biden won over eighty-one million votes, more than any candidate had ever received in the history of the United States. Donald Trump got seventy-four million votes, which was the most votes for any sitting president, but not enough to beat Biden.

Since many people had mailed their ballots, it took a while to count all the votes. The Trump campaign contested many of the elections, especially in areas where mostly Black people had voted. In some cases, the Republicans even tried to keep the elected Democratic politicians from taking office.

Even though the presidential race had been decided, another voting battle was brewing right in

Stacey Abrams's home state of Georgia. Because the two Georgia Senate races had been so close, they needed to have a runoff or tiebreaker election. If the two Democratic senators won, it would mean that the United States Senate, which has been majority Republican for more than five years, would be evenly split instead. And if there was a tie in the voting, Democratic Vice President Kamala Harris could cast the final vote to break the tie. So if the Republicans lost both Senate races in Georgia, they would lose their power in Congress, since there were already more Democrats in the House of Representatives.

The two Democratic candidates for the Senate were a Black minister named Raphael Warnock and a young Jewish man named Jon Ossoff. Americans

from coast to coast wrote postcards, ran phone banks, and made donations to support their races. After the votes were all counted, history was made again—Georgia sent its very first Black man and Jewish man to the United States Senate.

Along with her supporters, her partners, and the American people, Stacey Abrams had done what seemed to be impossible. Fair Fight's outreach had turned the former slave state of Georgia from a deep Republican red to a bright Democratic blue. Her New Georgia Project had become the New America Project.

The presidential election of 2020 was called the freest and fairest election in American history. For the first time, more people in the United States were able to have a say in how they were being governed. Despite all the obstacles thrown by those who did not want Black, brown, and young people to vote, they were the ones who swayed the presidential election of 2020.

But as soon as the election was over, Republican lawmakers around the country began ramping up new voter restriction laws for the 2022 and 2024 elections.

So Stacey Abrams's work continues.

EPILOGUE

A More Perfect Union

"We the People of the United States, in Order to form a more perfect Union, establish Justice, insure domestic Tranquility, provide for the common defense, promote the general Welfare, and secure the Blessings of Liberty to ourselves and our Posterity, do ordain and establish this Constitution for the

United States of America."

When Stacey Abrams was just a toddler, this line inspired the chorus of a popular song on the Saturday-morning television program *Schoolhouse Rock!* It is the preamble of the United States Constitution—the rulebook for the American government. The song taught a generation of children about the founding fathers' promise of freedom and fairness for the people of the United States.

From a young age, Stacey also knew about the power of voting to change the lives of individuals, communities, cities, states, and the entire country. For generations, her family, along with so many other Black families and people of color, struggled for the freedom to use the rights afforded to them as citizens of the United States. Her great-great-grandparents endured the horrors of slavery. Her grandparents and parents fought their way through the evils of the Jim Crow South to bring voting rights to all Americans. So, when it was time for Stacey's generation to take the stage, she fought not only for her own political ambitions—she did it for her family, for the people of Georgia, and for people all over the United States of America.

Five Famous Black Women in United States Politics

Ida B. Wells (1862–1931): investigative journalist and early civil rights and women's rights leader

Shirley Chisholm (1924–2005): the first Black woman elected to the US Congress, the first Black candidate for a major party's nomination for president of the United States

Barbara Jordan (1936–1996): the first Black woman from the South to serve in the US House of Representatives

Kamala Harris (1964–): California attorney general, California US Senator, and the first Black, South Asian, and/or female vice president of the United States

Michelle Obama (1964–): attorney, author, advocate, and the first African American First Lady of the United States

Service was always an important part of Stacey Abrams's life. Making sure that every American has the right and the ability to vote has been her ministry. Through her work, Stacey encouraged millions of Americans to believe in the power of their own voices. She showed them that their votes mattered. She showed them that their lives, their struggles, their hopes, and their dreams mattered. She showed the people of the United States that working together for free and fair elections could change the course of history.

After the elections, a talk show host asked Stacey what she would do next. There was talk of her running for the presidency. Plus, she'd

been nominated for a Nobel Peace Prize for promoting nonviolent change through the power of the vote. Stacey shared that she was finally going on vacation. She planned to read a stack of books and maybe watch some television. But Stacey could soon check one of her biggest goals off her spreadsheet: the May 2021 publication of *While Justice Sleeps*, a new spy thriller novel by author Stacey Abrams.

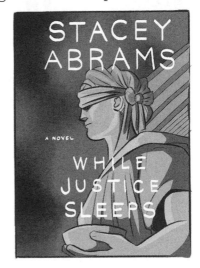

It took Stacey over twenty-five years, but she finally got there. She just had to stop and save democracy along the way.

Timeline:
Stacey Abrams

1973
Stacey is born on December 9 in Madison, Wisconsin.

1991
Stacey becomes the first Black valedictorian at Avondale High School in Atlanta, Georgia.

1994
Stacey becomes the first Black female Rhodes Scholar nominee to represent Mississippi.

2001
Stacey publishes her first romance novel under the name Selena Montgomery.

2007–2017
Stacey serves in the Georgia House of Representatives and becomes their first Black minority leader in 2011.

2014
Stacey starts the New Georgia Project and eventually registers over 500,000 voters.

1995

Stacey graduates from Spelman College with a bachelor's degree in political science, economics, and sociology, magna cum laude.

1998

Stacey graduates from the University of Texas in Austin with a master's degree in public affairs.

1999

Stacey graduates from Yale University with a JD (Juris Doctor).

2018

Stacey becomes the first African American female major party gubernatorial nominee in US history. She founds Fair Fight 2020, Fair Count, and Southern Economic Advancement Project.

2019

Stacey is the first African American woman to deliver a response to the State of the Union address.

2021

Stacey is nominated for a Nobel Peace Prize.

VIP Hall of Fame

Stacey Abrams is a trailblazing activist, but she's not the only Black woman organizing for justice in the US. Here are some other modern women fighting for justice:

Cori Bush is a nurse and pastor who has spent years fighting and organizing in support of racial justice and the movement for Black lives. She became Missouri's first Black female US congress-woman in 2020, where her experience as a single mother and formerly houseless person influences her work.

Lucy McBath is a congresswoman from Florida whose son was shot by a white man. Motivated by his death and by the ongoing epidemic of school shootings, she ran for office to fight for an end to gun violence in America.

Alicia Garza, **Patrisse Khan-Cullors**, and **Opal Tometi** are the cofounders of Black Lives Matter. After the  police shooting of eighteen-year-old Michael Brown Jr. in Ferguson, Missouri, in 2014, Alicia, Patrisse, and Opal organized BLM to protest the mistreatment of Black Americans by powerful people nationwide. Since then, it's grown into both an important rallying cry and a global network of activists.

Tamika Mallory is a lifelong activist who's fought for racial justice and women's rights among other causes. She is best known as a cofounder of the Women's March on Washington, which took place in 2017 and inspired seven hundred sister marches on seven continents around the world.

Bibliography

Abrams, Stacey. *Lead from the Outside: How to Build Your Future and Make Real Change*. Picador, 2019.

Abrams, Stacey. *Our Time Is Now: Power, Purpose, and the Fight for a Fair America*. Picador, 2001.

Cortés, Lisa, and Liz Garbus, dir. *All In: The Fight for Democracy*. 2020; Santa Monica, CA: Amazon Studios, 2020. www.amazon.com/All-Fight-Democracy-Stacey-Abrams/dp/B08FRQQKD5.

"Stacey Abrams and Janelle Monáe on the Fight for Democracy in an Election Season for the Ages," *Harper's Bazaar*, August 10, 2020, www.harpersbazaar.com/culture/politics/a33537366/stacey-abrams-janelle-monae-interview/.

"Stacey Abrams in Conversation with Holland Taylor." *92 Street Y*, April 11, 2019. https://www.youtube.com/watch?v=yEg07gU4Hi8&ab_channel=92ndStreetY.

About the Author

Andrea J. Loney won a Lee & Low New Voices Award and an NAACP Image Award nomination for her picture book *Take a Picture of Me, James Van Der Zee!* Her picture book *Bunnybear* was featured on the ALA Rainbow List, and her picture book *Double Bass Blues* won a Caldecott Honor for illustrator Rudy Gutierrez. Her work can also be found in the critically acclaimed children's poetry anthology *No Voice Too Small: Fourteen Young Americans Making History.* Her upcoming books include the picture book biography *Curve and Flow: The Elegant Vision of LA Architect Paul R. Williams.*

A second-generation Girl Scout, a huge spreadsheet fan, and an avid voter, Andrea graduated from New York University with an MFA in dramatic writing. She's traveled with the

Big Apple Circus and worked for the Walt Disney Company. Now she teaches computer science courses at a local community college and writing courses for organizations across the country. Andrea lives in Los Angeles, California, with her towering stacks of children's books, her devoted family, and their incredibly spoiled pets. Learn more at www.andreajloney.com.